LINKBUILDING
for Beginners

Learn how to build links and
improve your rankings

Thomas F.L. Storm

Link Building for Beginners

By

Thomas F.L. Storm

Book Description

Even though everyone have heard of power SEO strategy has and can have in the World Wide Web, it is never too late for enthusiasts and beginners to learn a thing or two about SEO that someone might have missed mentioning lately or in a long time. As the internet and what internet has to offer is changing, so do the rules of SEO and implementation of its techniques such as linkbuilding. With linkbuilding as our main topic we are introducing you with the world of SEO strategies and techniques, offering you lessons about basic SEO and linkbuilding, linkbuilding strategies and importance of backlinks and much more. You will find all of the topics related to SEO strategy and linkbuilding, covered in details through our chapters:

- Linkbuilding Basics

- Applied Linkbuilding

- SEO Analyzing Tools

- Linkbuilding Strategy

- Dropped Ranking

- Commonly Used Backlinks

Introduction

If you are reading this guide that means that you have decided to work on your SEO strategy that includes techniques for linkbuilding that will help you build your reputation, boost your traffic and establish a good name for your business or project. Needless to say that you are just at the right place and in the right time.

Let's begin with our lessons!

Who is Thomas Storm?

Thomas has over 7 years' client SEO experience in helping corporations and ranking his own webshop portfolio. His strong suits are link building with a creative, well thought out strategy. Thomas strongly believes in reaching out to webmasters and communities to build durable, mutual benificial relationships.

Chapter 1 – Linkbuilding Basics

Before you proceed with learning how linkbuilding is done in order to come up with and improve your Search Optimization strategy, for those who are still not completely sure what backlinks are, we are introducing you with linkbuilding basics.

What are backlinks?

When defining backlinks, it can appear that backlinks are no different than common links you use to get from one site to another, which is not far from the truth. However, the key to differentiate backlinks from links is to know that backlinks are actually taking you inside of a webpage as when you click on a backlink you would be taken to a file or the inside of a page the backlink is tied to. Still sounds like we are talking about links? Let us prove you wrong: when you click on a backlink, it will take you to the inside of a webpage the backlink is tied to, and when you click on an ordinary link, the link will take you through the outbound connection of the website page itself. This is the main and crucial difference between links and backlinks.

Why are backlinks important?

Now that we know what backlinks are, we mind as well learn why backlinks are important for your SEO strategy. We are going to present the importance of backlinks through graphical image:

Imagine that you have a blog about something and you know that there is at least a few hundred (more likely more) bloggers writing and publishing on the same topic. In order to establish your reputation on the World Wide Web is to get to the first page and this is where backlinks could help you. Backlinks serve as map pointers and as your blog is being connected with other blogs, the map is becoming wider, boosting your visibility on the ranking pages and increasing your chances for getting to the top.

Backlinking would then look like this: another blogger wants to add a reference to certain content on your webpage – let's say you wrote a great recipe and that you are blogging about food- the blogger will add a link to the webpage where that recipe is hosted. Whenever someone clicks on that link, it will take him/her to your blog post and that is a backlink increasing your traffic. In case the blogger had decided to put the link to your site, linking his page to your landing page that would be considered as a link, but the link leading to a particular part of your blog/site makes a backlink.

The more people share backlinks leading to your blog/site, the more traffic you will get and with more other blogs and sites you will be connected to – this will grant you better rankings. It is the same as in "real life" – the more people talk about you, the more popular you become.

Yes, you can always link your site to other sites by yourself and use social networking to lead people to your blog, but having other sites that are out of your control linking backlinks to your site is far more precious as people "move" across the internet mostly by using search engine or clicking on links – no one will type the entire URL address and search for your blog/site.

Importance of natural link profile

When we are talking about linkbuilding and backlinks, we cannot miss on mentioning the importance of natural link profile, but first we should answer to what natural link profile as well as link profile in general actually is.

Link profile is the overview of your web spot with the links and backlinks you are using on your site as well as the backlinks and links pasted on other sites. Google observes the importance and relevancy of other sites to the topic of your posts and content overall. One thing is for sure – you want your link profile to be clean and natural as Google loves clean and natural link profiles. Otherwise, you might even get penalties that will lower your rank and punish you even by shutting your site down; and that is what you certainly don't want to happen.

What is bad for your profile link is over-optimization when it comes to overly stressing out your anchor text, making it look artificial and irrelevant – almost as a spam, which Google consider it is. Also, linking your site with "bad neighborhood" sites will also make your rankings drop and your profile will lose on its natural look.

Now, what you should know is that in reality there are very few sites with natural link profiles – we are talking about great industries and online supermarkets that are trying minimally to draw visitors as their brand names are already established: think Amazon, eBay, etc. Instead of searching for a certain product, buyers will go directly to Amazon and Amazon didn't do a thing to make them do so: no PR-ing with links - people will willingly add backlinks to Amazon to their own sites as affiliates, reviewers or independent sellers.

You will have to work hard and establish your brand in order to do so, but till then you can try and keep your profile as clean as possible. Avoid bad sites, spamming, overly-optimized anchor text and fake web spots under your supremacy in order to put backlinks to your site, make your content natural and relevant, using only natural SEO keywords. Google will know how to appreciate that and you will progress as with solid good SEO strategy.

Now that you are familiar with SEO linkbuilding basics and some of your questions are answered, we can move onto another lesson - applying linkbuilding.

Chapter 2 – Applied Linkbuilding

In order to understand SEO and linkbuilding, you have to learn and practice. Below you will find explanation on some of the important points of linkbuilding you can and should apply on your SEO strategy in order to increase your visibility and head to the top.

What is Link Strength and How to achieve it?

Your link is strong if you make it strong – the link strength is measured by relevancy of the site where it's being pasted. We have already talked about what backlinks are and we have already mentioned a few things you should never do if you want to keep your link profile flawless or at least close to flawless. But now we are teaching you what to do in order to make your link valuable, i.e. strong.

You know that your blog/site is getting stronger and more visited if there is more inbound links, i.e. backlinks linked to your web spot, but how to achieve that and make your link strong and relevant at the same time?

You can't make people paste a link on their site to lead the visitors to your site unless the administrator or a blogger decides to do so as your site is relevantly important to their post – which is less likely to happen enough times to make your traffic bloom, but you can paste and share your backlinks through comments on other people's sites and blogs.

Not to make it selfish and intrusive, you should take care of making backlinks to your site if the situation calls for it. What wouldn't be good is to comment on any post just so you could paste your link besides the post – you are more likely to be marked as spam and banned from the site.

So, everything is about participating – you can reply and start conversations under comment area on blogs similar to yours and share your links, backlinking smartly and strategically, avoiding being a spammer and get banned.

Your links are then relevant and strong and the more of those strong and smart links you have, the bigger is your link map and the greater are the chances the search engine will love you.

Number of Incoming Links per Domain

When measuring your link strength, you should know where to look into in order to check whether your link profile is strong or not. First thing, you will check the number of backlinks or inbound links you have leading towards your site. You can do that over dashboard analyzes on your site/blog. The greater the number on the screen, the better – well, not exactly. Here is why:

You can have, let's say 2000 links leading to your site, but that is not what can honestly show whether your link profile is strong or not. Why? It's simple – the case is that backlinks can be easily faked and pasted on any blog or sit6e without being actually relevant – you can post them yourself, right?

What is important when measuring the strength of your link profile is to check the number of unique domains? It is very important to follow up with how many links had been posted to your site per domain. The more unique domains you have in your statistics, the better.

Let's say you have 2000 links across 200 unique domains – you should rather consider the number of unique domains as a true measure of your link profile strength. That is because a drop off can occur in case there are many links leading to your site on a single unique domain. We will discuss the dropped ranking later through our guide.

When posting with backlinks, you should also pay attention to anchor text, relevancy o9f the site or blog you are posting on and number of other factors that affects the link strength.

When comparing and analyzing the number of links and the number of unique domains, you should try your best to have that number close to even. 2000 for links and 200 for unique domains are not as great result as you might have thought at first. You sho8uld work on at least having ratio 2000:1000 as for example 2 backlinks per 1000 different sites relevant to content of your site.

Variation of Anchor Text

For those who are not yet familiar with the term anchor text, anchor text is a hyper link, clickable text you can use for SEO strategy. Just as with backlinks, keywords and links overall, there are bad and relevant anchor texts.

You've probably seen anchor texts everywhere around different sites. So if we, let's say, create an anchor text that says: "Click HERE!" that is a basic example of fairly bad anchor link. Relevant anchor text should tell the visitor what he is getting if he clicks. So, let's say a visitor is looking for advice on SEO strategy and he is looking over your backlink. Your anchor text shouldn't say: "Click HERE!" or "Click NOW!", but should rather say: "SEO Strategy" or "SEO Strategy Tips". The anchor text is actually a disguised backlink and will take the visitor to the page linked to the anchor text.

When it comes to anchor text, variation is very important. Why? You need to use different keywords when creating anchor text and every keyword should be relevant. If you are sharing information on SEO strategy, your anchor text shouldn't and won't say: dogs for sale or something absurd that has no sense with what you are offering through your content. All keywords used for anchor text have to be relevant and cleverly used. That is why variance is important.

It is recommended not to use overly-used and commonly repeated keywords – you have to try and be as imaginative and creative as possible, making different variations on the same topic, also taking care that your keywords used in anchor text are unique and less commonly used by yourself and others. Having variance in your anchor text is a huge plus when it comes to positive traffic towards your site or blog.

I strongly encourage you to read the free Anchor Text Bible written by SEO expert Daniel Gotch:
https://www.gotchseo.com/anchor-text/

Dofollow, Nofollow, Canonical and Disallow

If you are new to the SEO strategy world, you probably don't know or don't exactly understand what the terms listed above mean. We will explain it all to you shortly starting with the point and relevancy of the terms we have dedicated this paragraph to.

So, let's start with Nofollow – this is the attribute that can help administrators to basically mark a comment as a spam and with that done they are signalizing that they cannot grant for the content posted on their site. This means that Google might not take your backlink into option when it comes to9 ranking, but as Google has a crawler developed for this purposes only, your backlink can be taken into consideration. Now, even though a site uses Nofollow in order to block your link a way, they are forgetting that they are also sending a sign to Google that they have content on their site they cannot vouch for and this bad for their reputation in the "eyes" or search engine. That is why you should consider not using this attribute on your own site.

Dofollow is quite the opposite and the more dofollow backlinks you have on different unique sites, the greater are the chances that your traffic will jump up, consequently boosting your rank at search engines. If attributes are not set on any other mode such as Nofollow attribute, your backlink will be automatically considered to be Dofollow and Google will count it as relevant, adding points to your visibility – of course many factors will be considered, such as relevancy of the site that holds backlinks to your site, anchor text variation, etc.

Canonical attribute is created to help you make sure there is no duplicate content when it comes to backlinks from and to other sites and it is pretty usefully responding to the purpose it was created for.

Disallow attribute serves for blocking robot.txt – spammers with automated messages that might or might not contain backlinks in its content.

Next we are teaching you everything you need to know about analytics tools. Follow up with the next chapter to find out more about SEO analyzing tools.

Chapter 3 – Analyzing Tools

SEO Analyzing tools serve its purpose of helping you analyze your own and link profiles of your competitors. There is a variety of different analyzing tools and checkers, but we have compiled our own list to help you make your decision.

Ahrefs – SEO and Backlink Analyzing Tool

This is a fairly solid SEO tool as it comes with great number of features that should help you do your analyzes with minimal effort. What is good about Ahrefs is that its creators seemed to have thought about every aspect of SEO analyzes as they were making Ahrefs tool.

What you will get with this tool is a common backlink checker that will allow you to follow up with all your backlinks as well as with backlinks of your competitors as Ahrefs can smartly "hunt down" similar content as yours and help you check what your competition is up to also focusing on comparing your progress with progress of your competitors. You can use filters to find the most relevant content and check backlinks and anchor text for any website – everything you need is their URL address.

You can also use Ahrefs to find out what kind of keywords your competitors are using in search and whether they have paid backlinks and ads, as well as which one of their pages is getting the highest traffic. As a big plus you are also getting features such as crawler reports and position tracker. This will allow you to follow up with your ranking and your progress in real time as you will be getting reports on your traffic. With crawler reports you get your own crawler similar to the one Google has and it will help you track down and fix all the faultiness and issues that might be affecting your visibility and positive traffic.

Majestic – Backlink Analyzer

Since majestic is not working via third party, but it has its own crawlers, it is truly one of the few tools of this type. Majestic will help you analyze and pick up every aspect of a good SEO strategy, helping you analyze Anchor texts, URLS, keywords and backlinks linked from others to your site.

Majestic plug-in is also working on analyzing pages, ranking pages for relevancy and other important factors and grading them from 0 to 100 (logarithmic scales), that way enabling you of having a clear insight of which pages are getting the most traffic collected for your website.

It will also help you check other sites by analyzing their relevancy and ranking with use of URL so you could determine which site is good for your online reputation.

You will also get lists of 10 strongest Anchor texts and 10 strongest backlinks with simple analyzes performed by Majestic.

Majestic also offers two important SEO metrics for analyzing a websites link profile: Citation Flow and Trust Flow.

Citation flow on the other hand is a approximation (logarithmic scale of 1 to 100) of the average link strength (e.g. link juice) the incoming links of the analyzed website receives. The higher the better. This metrics has the most in common with Google's former PageRank metric.

Trust Flow is a metric that give you an approximation (logarithmic scale of 0 to 100) of the average trust that the incoming links of the analyzed website receives. Trust is calculated based on several factors, like where the website has been hosted (is the IP-adress and C-class trusted or notorious?). The higher the trust the better quality a link from the analyzed website can be for your Google rankings.

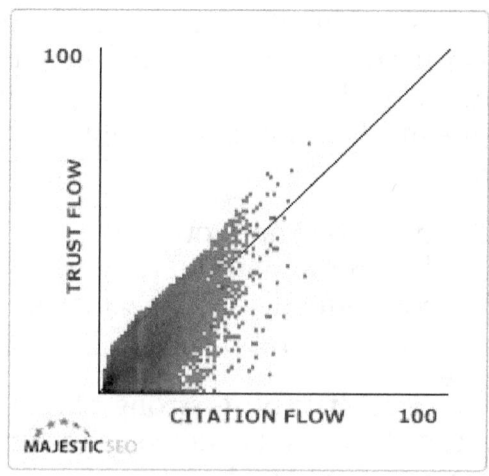

Recently Majestic introduced Topical Trust Flow. This tool gives you insight in the specific relevance spread of incoming links. For instance a website on running would or better said should receive it's majority of incoming links from websites on the same topic or semi-relevant topics like other sports or health related topics. When a website receives a lot of links from non-relevant sources this would be seen as unnatural and Google will notice it as well.

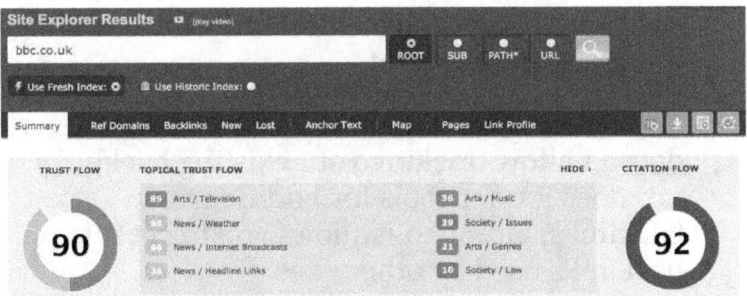

Market Samurai - Backlink Analyzing

This SEO tool is one of the most popular tools of that type, but unlike the two competitors' tools we reviewed for you, Samurai is not that versatile when it comes to all the aspects of a good SEO strategy – meaning it won't be as effective with analyzing your competitors and URLS as the previous two tools we have listed above.

However, if you are looking for a perfect SEO keyword tool, you will be thrilled with Samurai as this tool is almost flawless in analyzing and finding best keywords for your backlinks, anchor text and content.

This is the case for Samurai is drawing its information about effective keywords from Google keyword tools, that way finding the best value in keywords – this is more than effective for your SEO strategy as keywords and the choice of great keywords is one of the crucial points you have to have checked when building a solid good SEO strategy.

The downside of Samurai is that this tool doesn't allow tracking your existing backlinks nor does it offer tools for building new backlinks, although it allows you to get info on backlinks used by other sites.

Moz – SEO and Backlink Analyzer

Moz got its name because its creators are rather focusing on analyzing how trusted a link is or deciding whether a link place should be trusted or not, unlike other tools that mostly focus on analyzing backlink popularity. To add more value to your analyzes, you can also add Moz Rank – this extension will allow you to check on your backlink rankings while Moz Trust will be "seeding" trustworthy backlinks, such that are accepted on government and university web pages.

This will help you gain more natural backlinks, preventing dropped ranking and negative points.

You can run a checkup of your and other link profiles, getting detailed analyzes as Moz Trust and Moz Rank shows you whether certain backlinks are to be trusted or not as well as helping you determine whether yours and other link profiles are bad or relevant. Moz Trust is focused rather on determining trustworthiness of a site rather than analyzing its popularity in accordance with number of visitors the site is getting, so you might find this tool a bit incomplete when it comes to picking SEO tool analyzers. On the other side, you can always pair your Moz Trust with Moz Rank and add it on the shared dashboard in order to get 2 in 1 effect and be able to test, both, trustworthiness and popularity of URLS you are interested in analyzing.

Moz also offers two important metrics for analyzing a websites link profile: Page Authority (PA) and Domain Authority (DA). Page Authority is an approximation (by Moz) on the strength of a specific page based on several factors like incoming link juice and trust factors. Domain Authority is an approximation of the authority of a website as a whole. For ranking in Google improving a websites authority is very important.

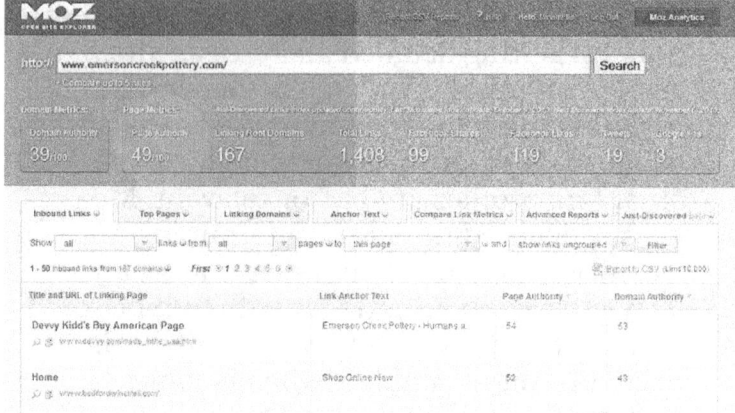

I personaly always analyze potential link opportunities on their relevance with Majestic's Topical Trust Flow, look at their average link juice (Citation Flow) and average trust (Trust Flow) and compare it with Moz's Page and Domain Authority to be sure that a potential link is worth going after. Better safe than sorry in my opinion.

Gillis van den Broeke of 90Digital.com researched the correlation coefficient between Moz' Domain Authority and Majestic' Trust Flow metric and found a 0.82 significant correlation! See here for their post about their investigation: http://90digital.com/reports/majestic-trust-flow-moz-domain-authority-for-seo-5520.html

Now that you are introduced to purpose of SEO analyzing tools, we can proceed to the next chapter and guide you through building your own SEO strategy that will help you establish

your brand and boost positive traffic to your
site.

Chapter 4 – Linkbuilding Strategy

Everything you've been learning by far was leading towards the point of making your own SEO strategy that is ought to help you increase your ranking and boost positive traffic towards your site or blog, leading more visitors to your web spot in a natural and clever way. Here is the main point you should consider when making your own Linkbuilding strategy.

Making a Plan

Every great strategy requires a solid good plan. In order to start off with working on your strategy, you should first get your own team – note that there will be plenty of work if you are planning on doing everything by yourself, although you can always rely on a good SEO analyzing tool to help you out with your planning.

Starting from content on your site, to make a good site in the eyes of crawlers checking on your website and determining what your rank should be, you first need to know that your content should never be categorized as spam – you need to use original content that is relevant to the subject of what your blog or site is about – you should never use random keywords only to draw visitors from different targeted audiences. Relevancy and uniqueness is the key for successful web content.

Make sure that your content is also optimized with proper keywords. Keywords should be naturally and without intrusion be equally spread through content and not overly-optimized. Researching keywords should also be your priority as you will use keywords for creating anchor text as well. Make your keywords relevant and as unique as possible.

Now that you have that covered up and you are sure that your content is completely relevant and not created in purpose of solely driving traffic to your site, you can focus on other points of your plan.

If you need help with researching and an extra hand for working on site, you can always hire content writers and SEO agents. Make sure you determine the budget and time needed for making your plan come to life. Consider hiring SM managers as well if you can't do socializing by yourself.

You would also need to use various social networks where you can connect with potential visitors and share your content.

To make an even greater outreach to all your visitors and those who are categorized as your potential visitors, you can offer free newsletters with relevant content. You will be sending newsletters via e-mail and keep your visitors up-to-date, which is another great way of keeping your visitors engaged and keeping your visits go up.

Above all you should be focused on planning your backlinking and driving visits to your site across other sites, that way creating a wide map of backlinks leading to your site – your links must be relevant, spam-free and accepted by other sites in order to make a natural link profile and a clear path for your SEO strategy – even better case scenario, the perfect case scenario actually, would be to have other sites posting backlinks to your sites, which can also be one of the main points of your SEO strategy.

Low Hanging Fruit

Another thing you need to pay attention to is the hanging fruit of the SEO. This means that we often focus on difficult and more complicate strategies when it comes to SEO that we often forget about simple things that can be performed and easily help us boost traffic towards our web spots.

One of the things not many administrators use is analyzing competitors and this can be more than handy as you can see what kind of content ha the biggest popularity, what kind of backlinks they use, how they use their backlinks, is their content relevant, how they use anchor text and what ki8nd of keywords they use.

This is also great for keywords researching as you also need to come up with original, but relevant keywords in order to drive traffic to your site by jumping to the top of the first page.

You can always use some of the tools we have listed to help you with analyzing competitors. Even though you will be looking up to your competition, always keep in mind that you need to be unique. This is a very simple strategy, but is very effective if planned out well. Sometimes the simplest solution that takes less effort is the best solution.

How to Compel to Sites to back you up with Backlinks?

We have already mentioned, and more than several times, that you can use backlinks on other sites in order to connect your site to other sites, preferably to web spots relevant to your niche. But, what you should be aiming for is to have other sites post backlinks by themselves that will lead their visitors straight to you.

You are of course interested in getting as many different unique domains as possible, so rather than getting 10 links on one site, you should focus on getting at least one backlink on 10 different unique domains.

But, how are you going to compel to other site to post your backlinks?

There are several ways of doing so and one of the ways is to connect with people from your niche that are your competition but are open for cooperation. You can connect with several different sites from your branch and try and make a deal of sharing backlinks across different posts where they would be posting backlinks to your site and vice versa. The more relevant sites you are connected to and the more unique domains you connect with, the better.

Another way is to use a true bless when it comes to marketing and connect with potential visitors across social networks. As you might have noticed, many people have their own blogs now, so you might stumble upon a blogger who appreciates your causes and goals then shares a backlink to your site. The more fans you have, preferably blogging fans, greater are the chances that you will get natural and free backlinks.

Backlinks can be bought, but it is not advised to do so as it can lead to drop off with ranking. You can find out more about dropped ranking in the Chapter 5.

Be Proactive!

Being proactive in the sense of SEO strategy is also a wide term as you need to be active and proactive in every aspect of your plan in order to make the entire mechanism work.

You should definitely consider being active on different social networks as you can easily get your backlink shared, also increasing traffic towards your site solely by being active on social networks. You will also need to dedicate serious time for analyzing and researching the progress you are making or not making. If there is no progress, in terms of being proactive you should work on tracking the problem down and solving it to prevent negative points or decrease in your ranking or traffic.

Be active and try to connect with other site owners and administrators from your branch and try and make a partnership. Be active in analyzing your competitors and always try to be innovative whether we are talking about coming up with original keywords or changing your strategy to better. Being active with changing and renewing content on your website, also blogging daily and proactively will positively affect your ranking and help you establish your brand. Once you come to that point, you will learn that obtaining a natural link profile is far easier when you have your brand established and well-known for a solid good reputation.

Heads up! Keep up with your competitors and follow up with your progress, always being ready to fix and improve something.

Get Your Reward with Altruism

In the spirit of sharing, you should be open for a sense of altruism where you should be also posting backlinks to other sites through your posts and content whenever there is a situation calling for that, just like you could have a good use of someone else deciding to share a backlink to your site.

If you are using reference from someone else's site, make sure you link their post to yours with a smart use of anchor text, that way leading traffic to their site. You get nothing from that, that is true, but what is potentially hidden there is a cooperation as the other party may return the "favor" in the same manner and post a backlink to your site as well as you have, clearing path for a useful "backlink partnership". Make references to various different sites from your niche by adding different backlinks when and if needed. Someone might return a backlink or two!

Leverage: Link Exchanging Options

Link exchanging is actually a thing that turned into a true network of users and participants as there are many sites and platforms specialized in connecting users in order to enable them to exchange backlinks. The process is simple and can be a good point of your own SEO strategy as you are basically posting backlinks on your posts, sending your visitors to their sites and attributing to their backlink map, whereas the other party does the same thing for you.

Note this: if and when you decide to get involved with exchanging links, make sure that you do a thorough research on any site you are exchanging backlinks with as you don't need your ranking dropping only because your backlink is posted on a "bad neighborhood" site. You also need to have in mind that you get less points by Google crawlers for reciprocal backlinks, which means that a backlink posted on someone else's site has more weight if you have not returned the favor – and in case of link exchanging you need to return the favor.

It might be easier for you to find sites ready to exchange links with you by signing up for one of many link exchanging platform, but it is recommended that you find trustworthy sites by yourself and make a backlink partnership without a third party being or getting involved.

There was a word about dropped ranking many times through our guide and that is exactly the main topic of our next chapter. Find out what not to do in order to keep your reputation flawless and your ranking only jumping up.

Chapter 5 – Dropped Ranking

No one who works hard on getting positive traffic and investing in SEO strategy wants to get a drop of ranking as a result to all the effort and hard work. That is why we are teaching you what not to do, stressing out all the wrong tactics one can get tangled in when performing optimization.

Negative SEO Factors: Why Not get involved with Negative SEO

Negative SEO does exist and can practically ruin every effort you have taken in order to boost, establish and increase your ranking. Negative SEO is a result to unethical SEO techniques some people are tempted to use in order to crash competition, that way boosting their own ranking. The point is that even though you might succeed in doing so – improve your ranking by sabotaging your competition, you are more likely to feel the other end of the blade as unethical SEO is indeed a sword with two blades.

There are plenty of negative things that can happen to your site if you try dealing with unethical techniques and enter the waters of negative SEO: your site can get hacked, spammy links may and probably will appear on your every page, the best backlinks you have worked hard for will be removed and the worst of all – your online reputation can be ruined making it hard for you to get back in the saddle.

There are a several factors that can influence negative SEO and you should in all cases avoid having done all of the points listed below:

- Google is working on tracking down, subtracting and identifying paid links – we have already mentioned that paid links might not count as eligible for good SEO strategy if Google tracks them down (and it most likely will). You will lose money and your ranking will drop off. It is always better to work on getting your backlinks by yourself than to have them paid for and then lost to Google's spiders.

- Another factor that can lead to dropped ranking is having your content duplicated – that is one of the mistakes you should never make. Google trackers don't count same content as relevant if the same content is spread on a couple of more sites. That means that even if you have two or three sites of your own with duplicated content, Google will count only one of them as legit based on content on your web spot. Make sure your content is original or at least properly rewritten if you are using other websites as a reference.

- "Bad" links – we have already discussed "bad" links and told you something about what bad links stand for. You should take care that your backlinks are not found on bad neighborhood sites, such as hate networks, porn sites and spammy sites. Google will consider you alike the sites you are linked to, so unless you want your ranking dropped, you want to have your backlinks pasted only on sites with established solid good reputation.

- Make sure every page on your website is crafted with attention to detail which means that instead of using a template to create all of your pages and page titles along with meta tags, you should take your time and create unique titles, content and meta tags for every single page on your website. Otherwise, your ranking may and probably will drop.

Overcoming Negative SEO Attack

Even though you have tried your best not to get involved with negative SEO techniques, it might occur that you become a target of negative SEO strategy regardless. What does that means and how you can tell if you are under an attack?

That means that someone is attacking your site in order to have your ranking drop and his own probably, in accordance with your fall, jump up – some of your competitors might try to take you down if you are "in their way" to the top.

They will most likely link your site to spammy and bad neighborhood sites, like gambling platforms and porn sites and have them linked to your site by paying them a couple of dimes in order to have your backlinks hosted on your site. Google will then categorize you as if your site was a bad neighborhood site as well.

They can use unnatural and irrelevant anchor texts that will lead to your site by creating new or replacing your own keywords that are relevant with those keywords that aren't. That can get you penalties from Google and your ranking will surely drop.

You can also get a virus leakage and become vulnerable with your personal info being possibly shared and on top of that your site will lose on its trustworthiness in case you get a Trojan or a similar virus. Your ranking will drop.

How can you tell whether you are a victim of negative SEO?

If you check the ranking statistic on your Analytics page and you notice a sudden fall that you cannot explain, that might mean that you are under an attack of negative SEO. You can also use one of the SEO tools we have listed and reviewed for you, like Ahrefs, and check activity for your website. New unnatural IPs appearing might also mean that you are under an attack.

How to Recover from Negative SEO attack?

Even if you weren't cautious enough, you can rely on a couple of ways of getting back on your feet and recover from negative SEO attack. Here is what you can do.

Link Detox

Link Detox is a tool that makes identifying and tracking down bad links possible. There are a couple of Link Detox tools and you can use any of them to make your search for bad links easier. You can always try searching for bad links manually, but it is better and more cost-effective if you choose to use one of the Link Detox tools.

Link Detox tool works by first performing detailed analyzes, going through your links and backlinks. After analyzing is done, you get all the info gathered and explained, counting over 90 different metrics. You will then get all the info needed on all the toxic backlinks that you need to remove as soon as possible. Not only that Detox Link tool helps you find all the toxic backlinks, but it also suggests checking on other suspicious backlinks that should be further investigated. Once you have found the toxic links, then you should get rid of them to "clear" your rankings and clear your site.

Link Disavowing

Google has created link disavowal tools in order to help the fight against negative SEO attack. Link Disavowing tools allow you to notify Google about certain companies they don't want to be linked to with backlinks. Sometimes, publishers buy links, as we have already discussed this option as one of the viral options of gaining on ranking by buying backlinks, so when they get penalties from Google as this action is punishable, they want to renounce those links and try to their positive ranking back with Google.

You can also use Link Disavow in order to remove links from bad sites after negative SEO attack and try and get your positive rank back.

I personaly recommend LinkResearchTools.com for researching bad links and removing them effectively.

This is a pretty useful way of handling problems with negative SEO and thus you should definitely consider using Disavowing in case of the attack or a mistake in your SEO strategy.

Google Penalties

The fact is that all of your hard work and well worked out SEO strategy can be wiped out through your website if Google decides to "ground" you for not behaving in accordance with the set rules of SEO.

There are two types of penalties and you don't want to see any of those near your site as that means that your traffic will drop – probably running your business and/or your reputation.

One of the penalties is Algorithmic penalty: this type works by algorithms and it affects more sites at the time, wiping hundreds and hundreds of sites that are not responding to the basic rules set by Google – that means that those sites will be losing their traffic as many (majority) of people uses Google as their search engine.

Manual penalties are also responsible for wiping down lots of web sites with almost half a million sites going down each month! That is a big number even for Google.

Many of the sites being wiped out are actually sites with spammy content and it is natural that Google reaction would be to return with penalty, but as we have previously discussed, your site can be affected as well if you happen to become a victim of negative SEO attack. That is the case scenario where you can get a penalty or more of them for being linked to spammy sites due to attack and in that particular case, you can deprived for near or over 90% of your traffic. If you think Google is only onto small business sites, you are wrong as even big business with huge name can and are affected if Google decides so.

Most Common Google Penalties

The most common penalties given by Google are content penalties, link penalties, over-optimization penalties and layout penalties. Each of the penalties has its own name and effects and you should learn something about the most common ones in order to recognize the symptoms of being stricken by one.

- Penguin – this is one of the most common penalties Google hands out if you are suspected to be linked with suspicious or spammy websites. It also recognizes generic anchor texts and suspicious backlinks that you might have paid. If Google considers your backlinks to be malicious or manipulative, you will get a Penguin penalty. You will get a note about from Google and you can also check your backlink performance in your Google Analytics. In order to lose the penalty if you get it, you will need to lose all the bad links that brought you in that situation.

- Panda – this is a content penalty and you are most likely to get one and lose your traffic in case your written sources are not trustworthy, relevant, important, are copied or overlapped and if you offer no value through your content to your visitors. You can get rid of this penalty if you decide to change your content to be everything opposite form listed above and wait for Google to forgive you!

- Layout penalty – in case your pages are overcrowded with ads and you have to scroll down to find the content needed if you are a visitor looking for the info you came for, then you will most certainly get this penalty. Google doesn't like websites that look like ad banners. You can still have ads on your website, but try to keep the number of ads as low as possible.

- Over-optimizing penalty – in case you have used your keywords more times than needed in a single blog post, you have just been nominated for getting one of these. In case you step up and make your site more crawlable, easier to use and navigate your over-usage of keywords will be overseen. You should also watch out and avoid exaggerating with SEO techniques. You want to add value to your site and not have it jump to the top by manipulating SEO techniques.

Now that you know what it means to have your ranking dropped, along with knowing how to avoid it and how one can get there, we can now skip to the part about commonly used backlinks.

Chapter 6 – Commonly Used Backlinks

As a simple guide for many types and forms of backlinks and backlink usage, below you will find brief descriptions for commonly used backlinks, so you could keep up with SEO techniques and learn how to make your SEO strategy better and more efficient.

Blogs

Besides from providing your visitors with relevant content, blogs can be a great way to boost your traffic if you know your SEO and if you are actively posting, updating your pages and informing your visitors. You can use your blog posts to reach out to a wide range of audience and "buying" them with quality and valuable content, you can have many visitors and other bloggers share backlinks to your pages, that way raising your traffic.

Press releases

Believe it or not, many people use press releases to have their backlinks spread by using press release web sites. The key of successful and spam-free press release with backlinks is to send it to the right source, keep it relevant and informative and use your links in a way that the news is truly linked to the relevant page(s) on your web site.

Comment linking

If you get involved in socializing with other bloggers or start researching, going through other blogs from your niche, you can add your backlink in the comment section (unless the administrator didn't ban it) and take the readers to your site – make sure your links and comments are relevant to the blog you are on and to your own content.

Partner links

Making partnerships in order to post your backlinks and have backlinks of others posted on your blog or web site is a nice addition to your SEO strategy and can be of help to others as well as for you. The more different partners you have, the greater are the chances that you will have a good use of posting your backlinks. Make sure you post backlinks of your partners as well and never make partnerships with spammy or bad neighborhood web sites.

PBN

Every once in a while a domain expires because the webmaster decided he/she no longer needed the site so after the domain is stopped being paid for, anyone can buy it for less than 15$. Expired domains have more authority so if you decide to build PBN (Private Blog Network); you want it to consist of expired domains. Private Blog Networks can be used to post your backlinks in order to boost ranking of your sites and other blogs. You just need to make the content relevant, connected, unique and original and then you can start exchanging backlinks with yourself and gain more than a few points with Google.

Web 2.0

For those who are not yet sure what Web 2.0 is, the simplest explanation is to say that any sites that are basically run and generated by users, when it comes to content, like YouTube, Twitter, Facebook, etc.

You can use Web 2.0 to post your backlinks in relevant context

Social Voting and News

By busing sites like Reddit, Instagram and similar platforms, you can reach out to wider audience, updating your targeted audience with news about your company/business/blog and get your posts upvoted and tagged. This will help you get more points and raise your ranking.

Q & A sites

Sites like Quora and Yahoo Answers can help you out with posting your backlinks as you can answer a question related to your niche and post a relevant backlink leading to a page of your site that offers proof or more answers. This is a great way of promoting your blog/site through your backlinks – just make sure the use of backlinks is relevant.

Social Networks

Social networks can help you keep up with new trends and new demands of your targeted audience. You can share your blog posts, news and announcements there and have your audience and visitors well informed, engaged and returning. You can also share your links and potentially have others sharing your links as well.

Directory links

You can link your site to some of many web directories out there and still play safe. You will certainly get your links spread out naturally without gaining penalties – you just need to watch for joining safe and secure directory, such as the one offered by Moz.

Forum links

Another great way of having your backlinks spread is to join a couple of forums related to your niche and participate in debates and conversations so you could post relevant backlinks that will lead to your site. Hundreds and thousands of people visit forums every day, so that means that you have potential visitors that might click on the link you provided – just keep the backlinks relevant to the subject.

Sitewide links

Sitewide links are links being placed on every page of the site, usually being visible in the sidebar. Lots of people are working on buying inbound and outbound sitewide links in order to get more traffic, but we don't recommend this technique in complete if you want your reputation flawless in the eyes of Google crawlers – buying links is unnatural SEO and it will cost you points.

Powered by links

You can always have ads spread across World Wide Web. This will of course cost you, but watch not to have your ads with backlinks leading to your site posted on spammy web sites just because it is cheaper.

Too good to be true, that's probably true

Black Hat techniques are all SEO techniques that can be categorized as negative and can add no value to your site but could still increase your traffic. You will most likely get penalties from Google and have your site set on being invisible if you try manipulating with anchor texts, create stuffed content with over-optimized useless information, share bad links, etc. Avoid Black Hat techniques even if you are craving to have your traffic boosted as like you have raised you will fall when Google gets you. Not recommended at all – in this case traffic is really one of those things that are too good to be true.

EDU and GOV links

Some SEOs are convinced of the positive effects of gaining backlinks from EDU and GOV sites because they are from authoritive government and educational institutions. To be frank, I do not see a lot of correlation between .GOV and .EDU links and higher rankings. However when measuring the PA and DA (Moz Authority metrics) I do see a correlation between gaining links from relevant websites with moderate to high PA/DA and increased rankings, so I would recommend you to ignore the specif domain TLD of a website and only analyze it's SEO metrics and relevance.

Conclusion

Now that you are a new lesson richer you can practice what you have learned in order to create and perform the best SEO strategy you can come up with. Make sure to stay out of the bad neighborhood and try not to get involved with paying your backlinks and making partnerships with spammy sites. You want to build a string reputation and boost your business by boosting your ranking. Linkbuilding can get you there and whenever you think there is something you need to be reminded of, you can always get back to our SEO Strategy guide!

Resources

50 Online Local Business Directories for Local Marketing

1. Google (http://www.google.com/local/add/businessCenter)
2. Bing (https://www.bingplaces.com/)
3. Yahoo! (http://listings.local.yahoo.com/)
4. Yelp (https://www.yelp.com/)
5. Facebook (https://www.facebook.com/pages/create)
6. Better Business Bureau (http://www.bbb.org/)
7. Angie's List (http://www.angieslist.com/)
8. Merchant Circle (http://www.merchantcircle.com/signup/)
9. LinkedIn (http://www.linkedin.com/company/add/show)
10. YP.com (http://www.yellowpages.com/?re=yp)
11. Whitepages (http://www.whitepages.com/)
12. Superpages.com (https://www.supermedia.com/business-listings)
13. Yellowbook (http://www.yellowbook.com/)
14. CitySearch (http://www.citysearch.com/)
15. MapQuest/Yext (https://listings.mapquest.com/pl/mapquest-claims/preview.html)
16. Local.com (https://advertise.local.com/)

17. Foursquare (https://foursquare.com/)
18. CitySlick
    (https://www.cityslick.net/reg.php)
19. USDirectory.com
    (http://www.usdirectory.com/)
20. Dex Media (http://www.dexone.com/)
21. BizJournals.com
    (http://businessdirectory.bizjournals.com
    /)
22. TeleAtlas
    (http://mapinsight.teleatlas.com/mapfee
    dback/index.php)
23. Discover Our Town
    (http://www.discoverourtown.com/add/)
24. EZ Local (http://ezlocal.com/)
25. Kudzu
    (https://register.kudzu.com/packageSele
    ct.do)
26. CityVoter (http://cityvoter.com/)
27. Manta (http://www.manta.com/claim)
28. UsCity
    (http://www.uscity.net/listmysite.html)
29. Local Site Submit
    (http://www.localsitesubmit.com/)
30. InfoUSA
    (http://leads.infousa.com/Landing/Updat
    eListing.aspx?bas_vendor=99862)
31. Infignos
    (http://www.infignos.com/addlisting/spee
    dlist.cfm)
32. Get Fave (http://www.getfave.com/)
33. My Huckleberry
    (http://www.myhuckleberry.com/)
34. Yellowee (http://www.yellowee.com/)
35. MojoPages
    (http://www.mojopages.com/biz/signup)

36. Brownbook
(http://www.brownbook.net/business/add/)
37. Magic Yellow
(http://www.magicyellow.com/add-your-business.cfm)
38. CitySquares
(http://my.citysquares.com/search)
39. Map Creator
(https://mapcreator.here.com/mapcreator/31.786427582245,44.322329,3,0,0?site=mapreporter)
40. Judy's

Book (http://www.judysbook.com/post)
41. TripAdvisor (http://www.tripadvisor.com/)
42. Thumbtack
(https://www.thumbtack.com/)
43. YellowPagesGoesGreen.org
(https://www.yellowpagesgoesgreen.org/)
44. Home Advisor
(http://www.homeadvisor.com/)
45. ShowMeLocal
(http://www.showmelocal.com/)
46. ChamberofCommerce.com
(https://www.chamberofcommerce.com/)
47. Yellowbot (http://www.yellowbot.com/)
48. Hotfrog (http://www.hotfrog.com/)
49. MerchantCircle
(https://www.merchantcircle.com/signup#step=stepOne)
50. InsiderPages
(http://www.insiderpages.com/)

286 Web 2.0 Websites

1. http://wordpress.com
2. http://xing.com
3. http://blogspot.com
4. http://issuu.com
5. http://blogger.com
6. http://wordpress.com/
7. http://academia.edu
8. http://livejournal.com
9. http://tumblr.com
10. http://friendfeed.com
11. http://goodreads.com
12. http://jimdo.com
13. http://storify.com
14. http://wix.com
15. http://myspace.com
16. http://weebly.com
17. http://salon.com
18. http://last.fm
19. http://sfgate.com
20. http://posterous.com

21. http://citeulike.org

22. http://my.opera.com

23. http://merchantcircle.com

24. http://www.merchantcircle.com/

25. http://www.wix.com/

26. http://www.tumblr.com/

27. http://www.weebly.com/

28. http://blox.pl

29. http://getsatisfaction.com

30. http://jamendo.com

31. http://technorati.com

32. http://blog.de

33. http://slashdot.org

34. http://bravenet.com

35. http://miarroba.com

36. http://angelfire.lycos.com

37. http://wikidot.com

38. http://edublogs.org

39. http://evernote.com

40. http://tripod.lycos.com

41. http://zoho.com

42. http://drupalgardens.com

43. http://blog.fc2.com

44. http://groups.google.com

45. http://newsvine.com

46. http://synthasite.com

47. http://couchsurfing.org

48. http://webs.com

49. http://wikispaces.com

50. http://keepandshare.com

51. http://youblisher.com

52. http://deviantart.com

53. http://gawker.com

54. http://diigo.com

55. http://box.com

56. http://calameo.com

57. http://www.zoho.com

58. http://angelfire.com

59. http://typepad.com

60. http://rhizome.org

61. http://tripod.com

62. http://www.tripod.lycos.com

63. http://rediff.com

64. http://www.yola.com

65. http://freewha.com

66. http://jumptags.com

67. http://rhizome.org/

68. http://blog.fc2.com/

69. http://www.zoho.com/

70. http://www.couchsurfing.org/

71. http://www.webs.com/

72. http://www.newsvine.com/

73. http://www.rediff.com/

74. http://evernote.com/

75. http://blog.pchome.com.tw

76. http://albawaba.com

77. http://dailystrength.org

78. http://datahub.io

79. http://hubpages.com

80. http://migente.com

81. http://redbubble.com

82. http://skyrock.com

83. http://netlog.com

84. http://twoday.net

85. http://blog.fr

86. http://travelblog.org

87. http://bitcomet.com

88. http://unblog.fr

89. http://kidblog.org

90. http://zimbio.com

91. http://allvoices.com

92. http://areavoices.com

93. http://ghanaweb.com

94. http://blogtalkradio.com

95. http://webnode.com

96. http://shutterfly.com

97. http://friendster.com

98. http://yudu.com

99. http://blog.com

100.   http://fc2.com

101.   http://bravejournal.com

102.   http://quizilla.teennick.com

103.   http://blackplanet.com

104.   http://dreamwidth.org

105.	http://blogsome.com
106.	http://moonfruit.com
107.	http://freehostia.com
108.	http://blog.co.uk
109.	http://soundclick.com
110.	http://quizilla.com
111.	http://squidoo.com
112.	http://zing.vn
113.	http://ucoz.com
114.	http://4shared.com
115.	http://buzznet.com
116.	http://eklablog.com
117.	http://rebelmouse.com
118.	http://snackwebsites.com
119.	http://travelpod.com
120.	http://wayn.com
121.	http://en.over-blog.com
122.	http://multiply.com
123.	http://hotklix.com
124.	http://sphinn.com
125.	http://care2.com

126.   http://doodlekit.com

127.   http://socialmediatoday.com

128.   http://dzone.com

129.   http://sitew.com

130.   http://wetpaint.com

131.   http://zootoo.com

132.   http://www.zimbio.com/

133.   http://www.blog.co.uk/

134.   http://www.dailystrength.org/

135.   http://www.shutterfly.com/

136.   http://hubpages.com/

137.   http://socialmediatoday.com/

138.   http://www.redbubble.com/

139.   http://www.sitew.com/

140.   http://www.migente.com/

141.   http://travelplus.wayn.com/

142.   http://blog.com.es

143.   http://43things.com

144.   http://centerblog.net

145.   http://crowdvine.com

146.   http://opendiary.com

147.	http://soup.io
148.	http://travellerspoint.com
149.	http://xfire.com
150.	http://thoughts.com
151.	http://journalspace.com
152.	http://jambase.com
153.	http://23hq.com
154.	http://devhub.com
155.	http://hazblog.com
156.	http://foroactivo.com
157.	http://forumotion.com
158.	http://wordpressy.pl
159.	http://kiwibox.com
160.	http://pusha.se
161.	http://snappages.com
162.	http://onsugar.com
163.	http://jigsy.com
164.	http://mouthshut.com
165.	http://mytripjournal.com
166.	http://blog.interia.pl
167.	http://sosblogs.com

168. http://doomby.com

169. http://blogbaker.com

170. http://20minutes-blogs.fr

171. http://filesanywhere.com

172. http://webgarden.com

173. http://bravesites.com

174. http://fotki.com

175. http://pdfcast.org

176. http://ipernity.com

177. http://yuku.com

178. http://diaryland.com

179. http://sosblog.com

180. http://webspawner.com

181. http://beep.com

182. http://blog.hr

183. http://blogdrive.com

184. http://gaiaonline.com

185. http://ge.tt

186. http://own-free-website.com

187. http://pen.io

188. http://tribe.net

189. http://spruz.com

190. http://cabanova.com

191. http://myanimelist.net

192. http://page.tl

193. http://blog.yahoo.com

194. http://www.cabanova.com/

195. http://www.own-free-website.com/

196. http://myanimelist.net/

197. http://www.spruz.com/

198. http://www.smore.com/

199. http://www.kickofflabs.com/

200. http://www.jambase.com/

201. http://www.asianave.com/

202. http://www.soup.io/

203. http://www.devhub.com/

204. http://www.sosblogs.com/

205. http://www.webgarden.com/

206. http://snappages.com/

207. http://www.webspawner.com/

208. http://pen.io/

209. http://www.doomby.com/

210.   http://www.blogbaker.com/

211.   http://unityfirst.com

212.   http://tblog.com

213.   http://experienceproject.com

214.   http://flixya.com

215.   http://geckogo.com

216.   http://mywapblog.com

217.   http://nexopia.com

218.   http://sailblogs.com

219.   http://exteen.com

220.   http://vefblog.net

221.   http://getjealous.com

222.   http://wallinside.com

223.   http://bcz.com

224.   http://maruta.be

225.   http://slmame.com

226.   http://ohlog.com

227.   http://soulcast.com

228.   http://workitmom.com

229.   http://manifo.com

230.   http://freewebsite-service.com

231.   http://iloveblog.com

232.   http://kazeo.com

233.   http://shoutpost.com

234.   http://blogskinny.com

235.   http://zoomgroups.com

236.   http://yousaytoo.com

237.   http://20six.co.uk

238.   http://a-thera.com

239.   http://blog.wox.cc

240.   http://blogspace.fr

241.   http://postbit.com

242.   http://trusted.md

243.   http://bigcontact.com

244.   http://beeplog.de

245.   http://de.la

246.   http://docdroid.net

247.   http://fotopages.com

248.   http://freepdfhosting.com

249.   http://hatena.com

250.   http://jux.com

251.   http://postagon.com

252.   http://jux.com/

253.   http://www.ourstory.com/

254.   http://www.ziki.com/

255.   http://www.geckogo.com/

256.   http://workitmom.com/

257.   http://space.travel

258.   http://selfgrowth.com

259.   http://yourtrainings.com

260.   http://busythumbs.com

261.   http://friendsite.com

262.   http://blogigo.com

263.   http://bloggers.nl

264.   http://joe.pl

265.   http://purevolume.com

266.   http://bloghi.com

267.   http://awebcafe.com

268.   http://iseekblog.com

269.   http://insanejournal.com

270.   http://vip-blog.com

271.   http://inube.com

272.   http://sweetcircles.com

273. http://mymfb.com

274. http://iblog.at

275. http://bloggerteam.com

276. http://www.purevolume.com/

277. http://worldvillage.com

278. http://fizzlive.com

279. http://blurpalicious.com

280. http://greasy.com

281. http://uwcblog.com

282. http://mozello.com

283. http://webstarts.com

284. http://www.xanga.com

285. http://webstarts.com/

286. http://officelive.com

17 Social Voting Websites

There is no doubt that taking advantage of social voting sites is a vital part of your successful blogging strategy.

Here is the lists of Voting Social Sites where you can summit your article for other users to read and vote them.

1.Bizsugar - This is a social bookmarking and networking site for small business and medium-sized business owners and managers. It allows you to submit, share and vote for the best business information links on the Internet. Any story submitted will show in the live feed on Bizsugar.Add a couple of friends a week to your account to gain more visibility to your profile and activity on Bizsugar.

2. Serpd - A social site dedicated to proffessionals in SEO, SEM, internet marketing, web development, website design, and any other job that involves working primarily in, or manipulating things on the web! So what can you do on SERPd? Thats easy.

3. Blokube – This is a social voting site dedicated to professionals in Blogging, Marketing, SEO, SEM, web development etc. The ideal of Blokube is to promote interaction between bloggers by "voting" with each others blogs. Interaction that builds up quality comments and interactive discussions.

4. Facebook Like - The Like button lets a user share your content with friends on Facebook. When the user clicks the Like button on your site, a story appears in the user's friends' News Feed with a link back to your website.

5. Tweetmeme- This is a service which aggregates all the popular links on Twitter to determine which links are popular. TweetMeme categorises these links into Categories, Subcategories and Channels, making it easy to filter out the noise to find what you're interested in.

6. Stumbleupon - Helps you discover and share great websites. As you click Stumble!, we deliver high-quality pages matched to your personal preferences. These pages have been explicitly recommended by your friends or one of 8 million+ other websurfers with interests similar to you. Rating these sites you like automatically shares them with like-minded people – and helps you discover great sites your friends recommend.

7. Smallbusinessbrief - Benefit from the popularity of Small Business Brief by posting your articles. It's a great way to build credibility, get exposure and increase traffic to your site.

8. Tottlers – This is a website for parents that allows you to submit an article that will be reviewed by all and will be promoted, based on popularity, to the main page. When a user submits a news article it will be placed in the unpublished area until it gains sufficient votes to be promoted to the main page.

9. Earnersclub - Good for submitting articles that will be reviewed by all.

10. Roundersbuzz - Very good too just like Earnsclub.

11. Brewpoll – This is a place for sharing news, web sites and articles about home brewing, craft beer and microbrewed beer.

12. Plime – This is an editable wiki community where users can add and edit weird and interesting links. Users earn karma when other users vote on their actions. The more karma you have, the more power you have at Plime.

13. Killerstartups – This is a user driven internet startups community. Entrepreneurs, investors, and bloggers are staying informed on up-and-coming internet startups using our blog platform, where internet entrepreneurs submit their startup to see what others think about it.

14. DZone - This is a technology publishing company that produces valuable content for software architects and developers worldwide.

15. Digg - This is a place for people to discover and share content from anywhere on the web.

16. Reddit – You can share and review all kinds of interesting content on Reddit and it has the potential to generate a lot of traction.

17. NuJij.nl – Dutch social news voting website.

Last, but not least. The Best SEO Forums To Learn More:

http://www.warriorforum.com/search-engine-optimization/

http://forums.seochat.com/

https://moz.com/community/q

http://www.seobook.com/archives/000161.shtml

http://forums.searchenginewatch.com/

www.ingramcontent.com/pod-product-compliance
Lightning Source LLC
Chambersburg PA
CBHW060419190526
45169CB00002B/973